The UNSPOKEN SCARS

CRRYSTAL AGRAVAT

Inkfeathers Publishing
www.inkfeathers.com

The Unspoken Scars
by Crrystal Agravat
Paperback Edition

First Published in India in 2022
by Inkfeathers Publishing, New Delhi 110095

Copyright © Crrystal Agravat 2022
Edited by Lokeshna Bulani

www.inkfeathers.com

To all the women around the world,
who are struggling to find a voice for themselves.
This book will help you find the unique,
hidden voice inside you.

CONTENTS

INTRODUCTION

Thoughts that can't be expressed, yet linger in the mind, can often be penned in the form of poetry. The poet stages a new world using her ideas, making the reader the protagonist.

Before manifesting, my involvement and love for poetry had been an enthralling concept for me since my early days. It served as a pathway toward my writing career. Delivering small pieces of poetry by famous poets in front of spectators was an event in school in which I always liked to participate. My intriguing nature made me compose a simple poem which received a lot of appreciation.

Years went by, introducing me to different phases of life, making me strong and powerful. It also brought life into the inner poet in me as she was in hibernation since my early days. Being a psychologist, I keep healing as my topmost priority and through this; I shall set an example for all my readers. Over a year ago, I decided to share my collection of thoughts with the world.

I hope that all the women looking for the pain and suffering to end get towards the right direction.

BETRAYAL

Your betrayal made me strong
Strong enough to face my fears
If I can, even you can

—*Crrystal*

Cheated

Beautiful young girl
Long highlighted tresses
With black kohl eyes
Beaming with brightness and
The wide cute smile
With crooked teeth
Made her an angel.

Angel had grown her wings
She left her palace
With pride and prestige
In search of love and
Met her prince charming
Both fell in love
A little world was formed
Everything was perfect

But
Soon their little world started
To crack into small pieces.

Life started to get tougher
Differences emerged
Love became boring
And shadowed her life
Prince charming no more
Was her tranquil in the chaos
But he became the chaos
In her tranquil body.

Prince charming in search of peace
Knocked the doors of other angels
He found peace in their bodies
Priority and timings both changed
He started to remain happy
She saw a new glisten in his eyes
sensed something was wrong
But trust encircled her.

A new pair of shining black boots

A crisp white shirt

With straightly pressed trousers

He was ready, but she was unaware

With a ring in his hands and kneeling down

Proposed another angel

Leaving this angel with pain and a

tag of a divorcee for her entire life.

Fading Love

In the beginning,
Everything seems like a bliss
Everything seems so beautiful
Everything is so dreamy
The original colour is yet to unveil.

Differences start occurring
Ideas clash
Like turns into dislike
Now everything seems like a big mistake.

Dislike turns to hate
Foul words start to enter
and sometimes even hands.

Even the little details
which were once cherished
become a hindrance
become annoying.

Love turns into a compulsion
into a pressurized feeling
that must be fulfilled
The love has faded.

Domestic Abuse

Girl leaves everything

For the man she loves

For the man

she wants to live with

Her dream to have a perfect life

Shatters in just a glimpse.

Frightened, scared, and horrified

Sees her husband in a wild role

Disturbed by this

Tries to call security, police, and her family

But

Nothing works

She is trapped

Trapped by her own love.

Sobbing and begging
To spare the horrors
But this worsens.

A tear rolls down
When the mirror shows her
Destructed swollen face
Tries to conceal her wounds
On her face
In her heart
But
Nothing works
she is trapped.
Taunts, foul language
Becomes a daily routine
Love disappears
Making her a solitary figure.

Mental Stigma

Afraid to tell the world
Afraid of being judged
Scared of being different
Scared to lose everyone
Frightened of making friends
Frightened of loving anyone
Panicked seeing another episode
Panicked to get to the shrink
Fearful of being yourself
That's the mental stigma.

Façade

The world is a façade

Where lies encompass

Shadows betray

The glisten in the eyes

Transforms into dullness

The smiles turn into

Low spirits

The cheerful stride develops

Into despairing saunter

The effervescent syllables

Turn into despaired

Phonetic entity

To conceal

A layer of trust

And makeup

Camouflaged the identity

The world is a façade.

Broken

I am broken into thousand pieces
Yet, I chose not to speak
Hopes have been crushed
Yet, I decided to be strong
The world screaming at me
Yet, my heart beats for him
His eyes can't meet mine
Yet, I accept him with a smile
Fights grow intense and painful
Yet, I swallow it with pride
Adrenaline rushes in my veins
Yet, I stay still with him fine
Him loving other women made me cry
Yet, I wiped my tears
I am broken into thousand pieces
Yet, I chose not to speak.

Crave

A powerful desire
To achieve something
Hunger to achieve
Basic thoughts of a rapist.

On a lonely night
Zoe left the club sloshed
Blurry vision
Tipsy stride
Kohl smudged
Eyes swollen
Heart craving for some help.

With the hope of finding help
Zoe started to walk in an inebriated state
Spectors vision judging her
A black Audi swiftly stopped by
Windowpanes rolled down
His hand appeared, offering a ride
With a vague sight, Zoe caught the hand.

Examining Zoe with a deceitful eye
He made his first move
Placed his hands on her fair thighs
Zoe, sensing an unacceptable gesture
Got rid of the hand.

Cleverly, he offered her a drink
the pill was mixed with betrayal
Making her lose her awareness
He made his second and a final move
And a reluctant love was made.

Unaware and used
Thrown out of the vehicle
Poor Zoe was draped in
The trace of a sexual assault
Unable to hold her head high
Left the world, unable to bear
the crave.

Attention

Petite and lean
But a shining star
To her parents
Was Zara.

Folks fighting against
The world for survival
Unable to administer
Their time towards their offspring.

One dreadful day
The folks had been
Summoned to the school
Accusing the little girl.

"She is a thief—she stole it!" They said.
Folks with a confusing glance
Looked at the guilty Zara
Her gaze lowered; eyes filled with tears.
The school counsellor
With a sympathetic voice
Disclosed to them
A mental disorder
Known as 'Kleptomania'.

Feeling of guilt
Embraced Zara's parents.

Unable to face the society
Unable to stop her tears
Sat in a corner
An urge, a craving
Hands trembling
With fear.

Thoughts of embezzlement
Whirling in her brain
Her heart reminds her to stop
Confused Zara
Buried her head
Into her knees.

Months later
Because of the therapy
Zara never stole again
Able to hold her head high
Lived a better life.

The Doll

Wounds and cuts everywhere
Unable to conceal
Left a deep mark on the skin
The mark of defeat.

A Porcelain doll
Fair and rouge skin
Raised with utmost care
Careful not to break her.

A gust of wind
Warning of a storm
Entered the house
No escape routes.

The poor porcelain doll
Broken into pieces
Unable to gather
Unable to breathe.

Wounded doll
With blood oozing out
Unable to control
Finally let loose
And she "QUIT".

Separation

A tear rolled down his cheeks

When the father left his family

For the country he was born in

The loan to his motherland had to be paid off.

The soldier valiantly detached

Moving on with a brave heart

With a hope of returning back

But little did he know.

25

His little heart was scared

Wants to reunite with his family

The duty flashes in front of him

Overwhelming him

With uncontrollable emotions

Broken from inside

But

A smile flashes

Swallows his pain

And continues to dedicate

Himself to his country.

Lost

Eyes swelled up
Unable to move her body
Brain sending mixed signals
Chaotic thoughts hustling in her brain
Crying and for help.

Powerless to bear the burden
Feelings swelled up in the chest
Nobody to talk to
Nobody for look for
Completely a solitary figure
In seek of peace and some love.

Completely lost her control
Took out a shiny silver blade
Clenched her fist
Scars visible reminding her of
Failed numerous attempts
Placed the sharp blade on the wrist

Imbedded the blade and slowly made the move

Blood gushing out of her veins

And a smile appeared on her face

Making various cuts, she relieved her pain.

Swollen eyes wet with her tears

Tears combined with pain and joy

Nobody came to her rescue

Defeated, she closed her eyes

And a new morning

With fresh wounds

Welcomed her.

12 Am

Dark and silent night
Sky full of stars
An owl howling at a far distance
Crickets chirping nearby.

A faint light flickering
Indistinct cries could be heard
An inevitable pain
A woman crying silently
Made the heart melt.

Valerie, the girl in pain
Stood across the windowpane
Hoping to see the new light of hope
Hearing her mother's footsteps
Quickly wiped her tears
Decorated a smile on her face
And switched off the lights.

All the lights off
Valerie washed her face
Dragged her creaking chair
From the table across
Removed her favorite stole
Flung it to the fan
Gathered courage and
Threw her chair with the
Help of her legs
Oscillating, she finally stopped
Stopped breathing
And the clock struck
12 AM.

Burden

"You are a burden
Get out of my life."

On a fine morning
Tires screeching
Crushing on the gravel
Reached an old building.

He picked up her luggage
Talked to the supervisor
And admitted her to that place
Left without saying goodbye.

Unable to adjust to the environment
She poured her heart out
Similar to hers was another soul
Her eyes swelled but she couldn't share her pain.

Similar pain and despair
Brought them together
Both hoping to see their family again
But dreams shattering everyday
Accepted defeat and now hoping to see
The face of death.

This is the harsh reality of old age homes.

The Mask

A dark silent night
He stood by the bridge
Bitterness encircled him
Departed the goodness
And entered the monster
Who was breeding in him
For a prolonged time.

On the next sunny day
He prayed to Shiva
Anointed himself with
The sacred ash
Gained the blessings of
His parents
Led a normal life.

The silent night reoccurred
Contemplation of his next victim
Bloody red eyes
Fierceness and rage covered
The monstrous mask worn
Ruined many lives
Yet derived pleasure.
This is a rapist.

A Flower

A young pink bud
Surrounded by the leaves
A whole new world
Waiting for it
The bud blossomed into
A young pretty pink flower
Have turmeric yellow hues
Standing out.

Summers had arrived
Hot gusts of wind blew
Making it difficult for the flower
To remain stable
Moving with the wind
The flower swayed and swayed
Until it reached
A muddy swamp.

Pitiful pink flower
In the midst of the gutter
Laid with shame
Dirtied itself
It laid there for hours
Finally gave up and sank.

Waking Up

Waking up to a hot cup of coffee is a bliss
The perfect amount of milk
The rightly roasted coffee beans
A dash of sugar and cinnamon.
Blended with hot skimmed milk
Served in a white porcelain cup
With a freshly baked piece of cake.

This just remained a dream
For the impoverished public.

Speculum

Obesity a common issue

All over the world

Few affected, few don't care

The world looks at you differently

Everybody fat shames

Yet

The mirror gives a different reflection

A true reflection of the soul

The personality comes through the impression

That piece of glass understands the true self

A true judgement passed by the reflector

The seasons changed

The fearless turned brave

The weak got their voice

Still the polished metal

Showed its loyalty.

Evanesce

A blur silhouette
Travelled across the distance
Distant cries
Cries for help could be heard
Could be mistaken as an entity
But it was an expectant mother
Wandering for help.

With contractions
She set out for aid
Knocking every door
Not a soul heard her cries
With fading vision
And succumbed power
Knocked the last door.

It was the door of hope
A door of her genetics
The door was her cause of living
With a heavy heart and
Tears flowing down
The father held her daughter
Immediately sought medical help.

A mistake was forgotten
New family was welcomed
The father devoured the pain
Wiped the tears
Embraced the child
Love won the war
Ego lost its place.

Mirage

It seemed so perfect
Waking up to love of your life
Drinking your favorite coffee together
Visiting every single place in the town
Kissing in every place possible
So, I leave the place with his taste
Reminding me of him every time I swallow
Like blood running in my veins
His love ran in my veins.

Then destruction comes through
Comes in a beautiful manner
The scar left is invisible
But the pain in the heart
Is incomparable and inconsistent
Leaving the memories behind
He left
Left permanently.

I cried and begged but nothing worked
Contact wasn't possible
Closed all the roads of contact
I made a move myself
Reached his house
House decorated like a bride
Flowers hanging down
Lights sparkling
Chitter and chatter of guests
In the chaos I sprinted my way up
Unlocked the door of his room
A cold shiver ran through my spine
A bright light blurred my vision.

Suddenly
Everything was quiet
I could hear little cries
As I moved downstairs
The cries turned into wailing
All the guests dressed in white
Wailing..
As I moved closer to the group
Saw his picture, a brown garland on top
My heart sank, heartbeat raced
Everything started spinning

Nothing in my control
Lost my voice
In despair asking others
Heard someone say
"He is gone forever."
With flowers in his hands
A ring in his pocket
With a reconciling emotion
Took his favorite bike
Unable to wait
Drove faster
Unable to see
The huge truck
Collided with the bike
His dream of making me his
Left incomplete
Till this day
His presence can be felt
In the morning sunrise
His love remains eternal.

Knowledge

Woke up to an empty space beside me
This was once filled with laughter and happiness
What remains are plain white sheets of solitude.

A blanket wrapped around my body
As if it didn't want me to leave
It clenched my body with hope
Leaving me in confusion
The coziness pulled me back
Refusal dawned upon me
Lashing at me in despair
Wanting me to stay.

My sadness blended with the sheets of despair
Making me want to escape
Escape from the handcuffs of the melancholy
Join the rebels outside
Free and beautiful in their own ways

But again
I am pulled back
Pulled back by paranoia.

It has been days since I slept
No ways to escape this
Then came an angel
Of hope and motivation
Full of energy and cheer
Loved me with all her heart
Lead me into the jungle of ecstasy.
Its words made me feel as if I am on the seventh heaven
I was able to let go of the severe anxiety
Which burdened me like a burlap sack.

i entered the world of witty
A world of wisdom and smartness
Challenges at every mile I took
Mind gained consciousness
The neurotransmitters in the brain
Signaled the neurons
Giving rise to eccentric state of oneself
What changed life
Was the power of *knowledge* .

The Longing

I am sorry
That my heart longed
I am sorry
My heart made the poorest decision.

The night of doom fall arrived
Packed up my luggage
Stowed all the essentials
Whatever came handy.

Clock ticking past 11:45
With red light across the street
Imbibing my room, filling it with suspense
With beads of perspiration on my forehead
With a rush of adrenaline
Lit a smoke for myself
With a cigarette in my mouth and
Insanity in my heart
Took a pair of shears

Reflected myself in the tinted brown glass
Trimmed the lovely caresses
Gave myself bangs
Masquerading the original me
Grabbed my passport in my hand
Dolled up with my denim and black ripped tee
Hid my teary eyes behind black sunglasses
Diffused some cologne
Threw in my black boots
Glanced at the whole room.

And there laid the love of my life
Covered in pool of blood
With his heart still beating
The slightest mistake of his
Made him pay for his sins
I kissed goodbye
Covering my hands with his sins
Wiped off his mistakes
Took a last glimpse
Heard the sirens
Quickly made a move
Fled away as a free bird
Yet my heart longed.

Enslaved

Freedom is beyond her understanding
Freeing herself from the clenches
Makes it difficult to breathe.

With sweat beading on her forehead
Heart pounding to its limit
Made her teeth clatter.

The route of her liberation unlocked
Courage finally spoke
A gutsy decision made underneath.

The bride walked down the aisle
In misery and pain
Yet she glowed in the green wreath
Clouds of despair grew dark
The trees shed their leaves
Yet it was difficult to breathe.

The house of the bride on fire
The flames fuming in her head
Made her clench her teeth.

Leaving her in solitude
With her crippled soul
She cursed the wreath.

Blamed it for her anguish
The mourning for her husband
Made her anger seethe.

Tears rolled down
With a desire for vengeance.

Convincingly played the part of a widow
Freed herself from the clenches of the monster
Ultimately, she was able to breathe.

Love Story 1997

A murky period of darkness
Bordering physically and mentally
Engulfed in despair laid
The French beauty.

Her skin so smooth
Eyes so mesmerizing
Her black locks
Smelt as fresh as daisy.

But

The moon had its dark side
Brown skin cuts and scars
Showing the anguish and despair
Black locks cut in a weird fashion.

Was fashion to her
And to the world, 'a cry for help'
Pain crawled its way to her cheeks
Down until it reached her jawline.

Amidst the chaos
The princess found peace
In the form a knight
The knight engulfed her dismals.

Presented her a bouquet of roses
Concealing the pain from
The thorns he received
Sucked the blood.

Granted her happiness
In return a boon of cheerfulness
Gaiety and joy
Were endowed.

The French beauty and the knight
Swore to protect each other
In misery and in pain
Both devoted in each other
Forgot their destitute
And lived happily ever after.

Never Saw It Coming

My heart flipped when I saw you
Never saw you coming from that path
The way you turned around
Made my heart race.

Your embracement fills my solitude
You never left any path unturned
Made sure I walked with you
In your hardships and happiness.

You left me in awe
Wondering how one can be so perfect
Your flaws seemed flawless
Your curves seemed to cure me.

I still never saw you coming
Your dark hair mesmerized me
Your hands made me feel secure
And your smile made me feel loved.
Your care was out of bounds
But I mistook it as love
Your touch was lustful
But again
I mistook it for love.

I feel ashamed and guilty
Of making a mistake
Of trying to love
Of being immature.

The thin line between love and lust
Made me baffled
Both these four-letter words
fucked me up.

Brain played a trick
My neurons flipped
Shifted allegiance
Made me the culprit.

Scared and insecure me
Went to seek help
The shrink shrieked
Broke the news to me
It was borderline personality disorder.

Demise

Standing near the ocean
With fond memories in her heart
White chiffon flowy dress
Swinging in the direction of the wind.

The ecstatic moments flashed across
Back to the day when she declared *Kabool Hai*
With pompous joy and happiness
She began a new chapter in her life.

Little did she know about the danger
That hovered around her every breath
The newlyweds lost in themselves
Lived happily.

A month later

With a phone call in one hand
And helplessness in other
She desperately called people for help
Nobody bothered to help.

Finally got some help from a cab driver
Took her injured husband to the hospital
Regrets and tears both in her eyes
Continued chanting the name of *Allah*.

The hallway filled with silence
Only her humming audible
Yet, he could not be saved
Broken Alizeh wiped her tears.

Wore the white chiffon dress
Her investigative instincts could not stop her
Checked the crime scene thoroughly
Found something to give justice to her love.

Pakistan's terror cell quivered with the news
Her love had been involved with terrorism
Her brain crippled, yet her soul did not surrender
Craving for justice, Alizeh broke every handcuff.

Fled to Pakistan
Gathered courage and evidence
Went to the court several times
did not surrender.

The writer found guilty
Ambushed by the cowards
Fought bravely against the wimp
Protected his family
Sacrificed himself
Justice prevailed.

Misogyny

This world is filled with hatred
Hatred for you, sweet lass
The world will shun you
Judge you based on your dress
Make remarks that will hurt you.

You will have to stand up for yourself
Things such *"ladies don't raise their voices"* will be said
Your self-esteem will be publicly maligned
They believe world is under them
And so, they are superior.

They forget what it takes to be a woman
Beyond breasts and a vagina
Takes nine months of patience
A thousand watts of labour pain
Four days of bleeding once in a month.

This doesn't stop here.

The desperate stares in the marketplace
The taunts and foul words
Nagging of the males in the house
Young lad trying to protect her
Only because the lass is free from her clenches.

Patriarchal culture present since ages
Still continues in a new form
Patriarchs along with misogynists
A lethal combination
But the world is filled with them.

You took advantage of his love
and now karma hits you back.

—Crrystal

Long Distance

Two lovers apart
Each suited in a different time zone
One experienced the darkness
While the other, brightness.

Days passed; seasons changed
Yet they stood together
Fought every storm that blocked their way.

With distance growing, so did their bond
Growing with deeper love
Unconditional immense adoration.

A night that befalls the tragedy
A tragedy enough to destruct
The magic spell was broken

The storm ruined the lovers
Tore them apart
Life had been unfair.

The sad prince sat on the aisle
With on the rocks in his hands
And sadness engulfing him.

Saw a reflection in the pond nearby
A damsel to rescue with open hair
Distracted, he went to help.

Fear wrapped around her shoulders
The brave prince protected her
Took her to the safe palace.

Drenched in the heavy showers
Both started to undress
Lust grew in both their eyes.

The prince forgot a princess waiting miles away from him
Shattered her heart
Let himself sway in her lustful beauty.

The next morning had been much more beautiful for him
The beauty was wrapped under the sheets
Displaying her each and every curve.

Swaying again, he made love
Intense and passionate love
Sheets wet with their passion.
The princess saw the lovemaking
Caught him red-handed
Threw her ring on his face
Left the town with a smile
Yet her broken heart sighed
With happiness, "God bless him".

Abandon

You left me in the midst
Amid a starry night
My heart ached
My soul cried
And, yet you smiled.
I walked away from you
Left my soul broken
For you to break it
Further.
And, yet you smiled
And this time I smiled, too.

Torture

Could not succeed
Succeed in fulfilling his interests
Succeed in providing him bucks.

A choice had been made by me
Could not blame anyone
So, I blamed myself.

Punished my soul
Sculptured the scars on my heart
Drank the poison of love.

Tears rolled down
Too numb to feel the pain
Wiped the dirt.

Dirt of being guilty
Which soiled my dress
Gave a quick shake.

Many called me "heartless"
Survived the crucible world
Yet again punished me.
The toxic relationship
Gave the bliss and pain
Both at the extremes.

He tortured me
Filled my skin with
Red and blue markings of his hatred.

Yet didn't stop loving him
Yet he didn't fill his heart with love
So, I drank his cuss words
Just like his poison of love.

Departure

We fell in love with
an understanding
And departed with a misunderstanding.

Malice Love

Your love was poisonous
Yet, I decided to drink
From the chalices you created.

Your care had been toxic
Yet, I held it with care
Until my heart and lungs flared.

Your betrayal was torturous
Yet, I swallowed it
Along with my pride.

Your pride was my death trap
Yet, I allowed myself
To delve into it.

Hurt myself to the core
Yet you did not care
Lost myself in this mess
Unable to relive.

Your love crippled me
Yet, my heart cried your name
Crushing my soul into pieces
Leaving me alone.

Crying
Love feared me
And yet
my heart loved
you.

STRUGGLE

The struggle is real,

yet satisfying

—Crrystal

Roller Coaster

Life always gives its ups and downs
Sometimes gives its sweet and bitter fruits
Sometimes shuts the door, but opens a window
Sometimes gives happiness and sadness
Sometimes gives contentment, but gives pain as well
Life has always given something, yet it is unbalanced.

Life gives birth and death
Sometimes a painful one
The soul makes its amendments
Yet gets attracted to the adversity
Sometimes life has a lot to offer
But
Sometimes life has a lot to take.

Pain and misery always linger
Mind screams in silence
The body suffers in suppress
Heart longs for departure.
But
Sometimes it stops for the beloved
Sometimes it stops for another chance.

Eyes shedding water
Hands trembling, veins puffing
Pain handcuffed her, unable to combat
Surrenders to nature
So
Sometimes life's contentment, but gives pain as well
Life has always given something, yet it is unbalanced.

Him

I could have been anyone
In this modern-day world
But I chose to be
HIS.

I could have done everything
In this modern-day world
But I chose to do with
HIM.

I could have kissed anyone
In this modern-day world
But I chose to kiss
HIM.

I could have married anyone
In this modern-day world
But I chose to tie a knot with
HIM.

Yet, you stranded me
With a kid and responsibility
Single mother could have
Led astray.

Yet, kept my head high.

Act

Pretended to be okay.

But I am broken
I am shattered
My pain rises
To the brim of me
Tall champagne glass.

The bubbly drinks
Similar to my nature
As you left, so did the bubbles
Making me as still as tap water
Leaving the conscience behind.

I announced my progress
From the relationship
Hard and difficult to survive
Yet, thought about my future
Made my last move.

Held my head high
Wiped off my tears
Gasped for air
Faked a smile
AND MOVED ON.

Self-harm

For many years I tried to quit
Quit something that kept creeping
Led me into the dark forest
Illusioned me with the fantasy
Scared me with the dark shadow.

But

Soothed my pain
Gave me pleasure
Provided me ecstasy
Gave me an escape route
To my pain and sadness.

Helped me cope
Gave me the scars
Yet, gave satisfaction
Silent cries turned into
pleasure.

It engulfed me
Made me an addict
All control over me
Held me captive
That was my habit
Habit of "self-harm".

Dear Father

The touch I crave
Your care I still linger
The warm stroke on my head
Makes me twitch my fingers.

The feeling remains incomplete
Even if replaced by a man in my life
Thoughts flew in my head constantly
About the fear of being an inadequate wife.

When she is born
she falls in love with him
Gives him a crown of gems
Little did she know that
The hero in her life was already claimed.

Her eyes filled with tears
Swallowed her pain
Faked a smile on her face
As her efforts were all in vain.

Why stress about the person

Who doesn't even care to ask

"Are you okay?"

Patience

More the distance, the heart grows fonder
More the distance, more you will
feel loved
More the distance, more fights you will experience
More the distance, more tears you cry
More the distance, more is the crushing of your soul
More the distance, more misunderstandings
More the distance, more forgiveness will be granted
More the distance, stronger the bond

So, remember long distances are possible, just be patient.

He doesn't want you and if he does,

he will reach out to you,

so stop overthinking and stay happy.

—Crrystal

Forever

My body left you
Yet, my soul remained with you.

My hands left yours
But your touch remained forever.

My feet did leave your house
Yet your footprints remained endlessly.

My clothes did go with me
Yet your fragrance surrounds me.

We parted
But 'us' stays together.

Captive Love

Chained by love
You kept me tied
Left me no options
But to kill myself.

The pain seemed easier to bear
Once I slit my wrist
Your torture seemed worse
Then me killing myself.

I am dead
Thanks to you
But baby
I am going to haunt you
Cause' I am a nightmare dressed like a daydream.

You took one precious thing from me
That is smile.
But you gave me a valuable thing in return
tears.

Yet I forgive you.

Unleash

Your memory haunts me
It has held me captive in my dreams
Clinging it strong to my brain
Making me your slave.

Release me from your clenches
Uncuff my heart from yours
Bestow upon me my freedom
Liberate your love from mine.

Expectations

Expectations ruins happiness
Expectations ruins relationships
And ruins the last remains of the soul.

Once a little lass expected
Anticipated the rewards
Little did she know that
Dreams gets crushed
You get broken,
But
Young and naïve, cried a little
Contemplation of her gifts
Of her happiness and joy
Made her a melancholy soul.

A young girl and a boy

Both deeply in love

Both turned mature

the girl expected the return of her love in the form of marriage

Expectations ruined her happiness

And trust ruined her relationship

She never believed in love

Ever again.

A couple living in the midst

Of a crowded city

No time to spend

With each other

Always expected

something or the other

from each other

And ended up

In separation

What was ruined was their expectations.

With age grew their insecurities
An old couple had been
Destroyed by their own happiness
Destroyed by their own expectations
Of expecting their children to
Return their interest of love
But they failed.

Lesson learnt
Stop expecting
Start accepting.

One Day

One day I will be proud
that day will be special
One of a kind.

the tears rolling down my cheeks
will be of happiness
the eternal joy of hard work.

Newspapers will have me on their front pages
People will talk about me

Youth will be inspired
to be one like me
to have their own identity.

Some will agree
Some will disagree
But still, I will continue to make the change.

That's how a young president
A ruler, a game changer
Is born.

Love

A four-letter word
Changed my life
Society termed it as lust
I termed it as affection
His faith and care
Instilled in me
Made me desperate
His caring touch
His affectionate stare
Made me skip a beat
Still the society did not accept.

We separated
Situations made them so
Yet, we stayed strong.

The Yellow Petals

The sun shining brightly asked the flower

"I hope my rays are not hurting or burning you"

The flower turned towards the sun

Opened its bright yellow petals and replied

"Your rays provide growth to me

Your rays help me survive

Your rays are a blessing in disguise"

The sun intellectually asked the flower again

"Shouldn't you be worshipping me? I have given you your life."

The flower with a smirk replied,

"You have guided me and provided a push

But with the help of my poise

I am able to survive and confront you

I won't worship you, I will carry your blessings

And continue my journey."

Today we know this flower as

'The sunflower'.

I Still Love You

I look back how we met each other
Pleasant and sunny day it was
Cherishing the finest moments
Made my eyes teary.

Photos stored our love
Gifts stored our emotions
Our little abode stored
Our vibes and us.

I sometimes smile
Thinking about the dreams
We dared to fulfil
Yet, it still remains incomplete.

Change is inevitable
And so are we
I did leave you
But my soul didn't.

My soul aches for you
Screams your name
The pain is unbearable
Facing the pain
Made me stronger.

I sacrificed my love
My biggest strength
No more with me
Makes me weep
Tears of sadness.

Soul aching for his presence
Tongue wanting his taste
Hands missing his touch
Eyes lacking his image
Ears longing for his voice.

Shut the door for his love
Isolated myself from his shadow
My heart cried, yet put on smile
For everyone as they looked upon me
Broken and destructed, yet my face smiles.

Pain still lingers
Yet had to move on
Still hating myself
Started a new chapter
Smile hides my pain.

The Power

I am the lioness in the cage
Roaring with injured sighs
Lonely in the deep sea of
Sadness and pain
Wanted to break the cage
Weak, agile, and injured
Lioness roared for last time
Broke her shackles and
Chose to love another world
Chose freedom and left happiness
She wasn't supposed to be here
Yet she struggled her way through.

You left
But your memories didn't.

Value increases

Once they're gone.

I did fight for you
But little did I know
The fight was a waste
As you were the reason
Of this hassle.

Listen to my silence
It tells the truth
See my tears
It shows my suffering
Feel my pain
It shows my love
Perceive my broken heart
Manifests the agony
Bear my anger
It shows my fight
See my hatred
Shows my tolerance.

A conversation of a broken heart
and its emotions.

ACCEPTANCE

I am free.

The first rule in the book of love is

Acceptance

With love or without love

Beginning

Start a relationship
But with yourself
Fall in love
But with yourself
Let yourself loose
Live a little and give joy

Lonely

Make solitude
Your best friend

Make darkness
Your soulmate

Distressing

I know it is tough
Tough to heal
The wounds yet fresh
Screaming to be healed
Healing is difficult
But provides an eternal relief
Leaves the heart scarred
Making you an adult
You maybe be confused
You might want to yell
But remember,

"You are strong and
you can conquer."

Happily, Ever After

He left unimaginable wounds
Both physically and emotionally
Left me scattered in pieces.

Then came a saviour, a prince
With glistening brown eyes
Chivalry running through his veins.

Fixed the princess with his charm
Left her in awe when she landed in his arm
Magically eliminated her emotional harm.

As their lips touched each other
Felt each other's taste
Their breaths mingled
She felt the adrenaline rush
Heart raced as he expressed his
Undying love and so they lived
"Happily, ever after."

Mon cœur

Tu m'as volé mon cœur

Rénové avec votre humour

Tes yeux m'ont rendu fou

Ça m'a fait plonger en eux

J'aimerais pouvoir te dire

Que tu es plus que

« Mon Ami ».

[You stole my heart

Repaired it with your humor

Your eyes made me crazy

Made me delve in them

I wish I could tell you

That you are more than just

"My Friend".]

Impulse

Given up on love
Jinxed myself for the rest of the day
Wept tears and applied a mask of Moroccan clay.

Bleep!
My phone was adorned with a notification
It was from my crush
This was an utter satisfaction.

2433.91 miles away, home to my bliss
Distance played his tricks
Yet, he was mine in a flick.

Texting and Facetime
While we drank our wine
And together we dined.

We were so busy in our lives
Our communication had to drop
Yet we became each other's priorities
Our love always at the top.

Captured my mind
With his cheesiness
I grew fonder of him
And he filled my heart
With love to the brim.

Lies That Smile

Packed my tears
In a box of happy lies
The key in my hands
Frightened to open
handed it over.

My soul lost its existence
Made me a stronger woman
But snatched away my only right
The right to love.

Forgotten how to love
Strayed on the pathways
In search of someone
Who would call me theirs.

Little did I know
My bad luck would prey upon me
Would make me crave for even more
Heart sank even more.

Repaired my wounds with words
Saw happiness in others, found my key
opened the box of lies
The tears dried up left in me a hollow hole.

once again filled with happy lies.

Hopeful Light

Life has always been hard
Especially to those
Cursed like me.

Heard that God sends his angel
Speculation filled my mind
Thought would never be lucky.

Then the smallest ray of light
Shone upon me
Blinded my eye at first.

Then the light seemed to be perfect.

It brought me sunshine

It brought me laughter.

Sometimes the light and I argued

Had our differences

But it chose to be with me.

Soon the light of hope

Made me fall in love

We gave ourselves a chance

Then bloomed our romance.

I breathe not air, but stress
Life hadn't not been fair
Threw its worst balls at me

How I Met Your Father

Solitude made me ponder
Time to make some connections
Browsed the net.

Came across "Omegle"
Shy at first, hid myself
Connected with an artist.

Showed me his sketches
Felt that vibe with him
Gave my details and heart to him.

With his good looks and his talent
Took my breath away
Quickly captured his soul.

A cute Punjabi guy
Snatched my sorrows
Filled my life with happiness.

So proud to call him mine
Proposed me so fine
Put the ring on my finger
Proudly called him my husband
Children, That's how you mother
Met your father.

Him

In my pyjamas sipping through my coffee
Consumed my last toffee
Came a across a scope
Of 'Omegle', my only hope.

Saw a cutie with his sketches
In awe, made a move
Exchanged our numbers
As our feelings got approved.

He completed me in every way
That's how we used to sway
Accepted my every flaw
Which made my day glow.

This was just the beginning
He saved my reckoning
Feelings grew stronger
I was sad no longer.

Relationship evolved
Took a huge leap
From being friends
To lovers.

Selenophile

Once I met the moon
He was a bright one
Talked about his endeavors
His illumination blinded my eye
Yet, I absorbed his shine.

He led me into a whole new dimension
Blinded by his illusion
Walked across the path of thorns
Made my heart mourn.

Tears screamed at me
Silenced it with a glee
I felt something deep inside me
Struggled with it, but
I set the soul free.

At some point

You must stop

Stop searching for him

For his soul

Get closure not from him

But yourself.

Be Mine

I don't want to be just friends

I want you to be mine

Just mine.

Substituted

Heart broke into thousand pieces
Watching you taking those Circumambulations.

The promises made to each other
Vanished within seconds
Was replaced with another angel.

With watery eyes and quivering lips
Took a handful of yellow flowers
Gave them blessings as he became hers.

The dismal struck me hard
His memories made me stay alive
Made a little home of me
and him.

Memories

All my strength melts into

Weakness

Only in front of you

Resilient

When life gave me lemons
I made a lemonade
But
When you gave me a lemon,
I made a cocktail.

Life gave me opportunities
Let it hang loose
But
You gave me opportunities
I conquered the world.

There will be fights

There will be jealousy

There will be good days

There will bad days

But

Keep hanging on

Love will solve everything.

I am writing this thinking about you.

How you came into my life
How sorted it became.
Silence turned into hope
Hope turned into belief
Hatred turned into love
And love turned from "I"
To "us".

My sweetest memory
—Our first message

My favourite time of the day
—When I receive your call

My biggest fear
—If you leave me

My biggest hope
—I will see you soon

My biggest sadness
—Our distance

—Every long-distance lover

I love you can be said in
Different languages but
The feeling remains the same.

You might not be the Ironman to the world

But for me you are my superhero

You stood as a pillar
Took all the blame
Thunder shone upon you
Yet you remained still
Made me the best
This is how you passed
My love's test.

Victory

The sea inside me rises

Caused a big chaotic crisis

The world shall fear the rising waves

Yet the soul won't give up

Creating a fading phase

Forming an enormous grenade

Blasting into thousand little pieces

Picked up those until it scratched my fingers

Loved the pain that was inflicted on me

The deeper my scars grew

More the world got intimidated

Fearful world gave up

Giving my success a pump

The Remainder of You

The white waves crashing reminded me of the time
when love was fresh, as fresh as a daisy. The blue sky
was a constant reminder that love can be free,
but if controlled would roar into thunderstorms.
The salty freshwater smell was a smell for others,
but for me, a reminiscence of my childhood when
love was fresh, as fresh as a daisy.

The little flower

Plucked from its roots

Little did she know the

Garden around

Found herself bound

Made a mistake of mingling with thorns and got hurt

The garden blamed her, yet didn't realise her mistake, too late
for her growth.

The whole garden against her

Alone fought her battles

World taunted her

Changed and reformed flower

Tried to live a happy life

Yet the broken petals often showed

Her the mirror

Couldn't live, tried to get crumpled

Yet survived the entire struggle

The scars

The pain

The wounds

Her sacrifice

Her transformation

Gave her the power

To turn the words into weapons

Made a mark into the world

Introduced herself as an

Author and a poetess

ABOUT THE AUTHOR

Crrystal Agravat is a 25-year-old writer who found her way through the complicated field of psychology. Her fairy tale-inspired childhood gave her a chance to construct little artworks. Her creative imagination provided her the platform to express her thoughts in the most beguiling way possible. Inspired by Emily Dickinson, Maya Angelou, and Rupi Kaur, her world revolves around poetry. Her undying love for writing and expressing thoughts on paper brought her to make her debut in the world of poets. Her poems focus on sadness, love, betrayal, and hope. To her, writing is like the freedom a slave experiences after its banishment. In simpler terms, writing is a part of her essential existence.

INKFEATHERS PUBLISHING

We love creating beautiful books for you!

Come be a part of our ever-growing community of writers. Grow, write, and publish with us!

Scan here and get to know us better.

Connect with us on socials. We'd love to hear from you!

    Inkfeathers Publishing